Little Pebble™

Celebrate F...

Harvest Time

by Erika L. Shores

CAPSTONE PRESS
a capstone imprint

Little Pebble is published by Capstone Press,
1710 Roe Crest Drive, North Mankato, Minnesota 56003
www.capstonepub.com

Library of Congress Cataloging-in-Publication Data
Shores, Erika L., 1976– author.
 Harvest time / by Erika L. Shores.
    pages cm.—(Little pebble. Celebrate fall)
 Summary: "Simple nonfiction text and full-color photographs present crops and vegetables
that are harvested in fall"—Provided by the publisher.
 Audience: Ages 5–7
 Audience: K to grade 3
 Includes bibliographical references and index.
 ISBN 978-1-4914-6002-3 (library binding)—ISBN 978-1-4914-6014-6 (pbk.)—
 ISBN 978-1-4914-6026-9 (ebook pdf)
 1. Food crops—Harvesting—Juvenile literature. 2. Harvesting—Juvenile literature.
 3. Autumn—Juvenile literature. I. Title.
 SB129.S56 2016
 631.5'5—dc23   2015001841

Editorial Credits
Cynthia Della-Rovere, designer; Gina Kammer and Morgan Walters, media researchers;
Katy LaVigne, production specialist

Photo Credits
Alamy: © DP RM/Alamy, 9, © Universal Images Group Limited, 21, Gaertner, 5; Capstone Studio:
Karon Dubke, (dirt texture) 20, 21, 22, 23, 24; Dreamstime: Anthony Aneese Totah Jr., 6; Glow
Images: Corbis/© David Frazier, cover; Shutterstock: aquariagirl1970, 3, 24, cocozero, 18, 19,
Dancake, (dots on border) throughout, Denis and Yulia Pogostins, 13, Elena Schweitzer, (different
vegetables) throughout, I love photo, 15, MNStudio, 16, Monkey Business Images, 10, 11,
stefan11, 1, 8, Vaclav Volrab, (corn on the cob) throughout

Table of Contents

On the Farm 4

In the Garden 10

Glossary 22
Read More 23
Internet Sites . .23
Index 24

On the Farm

Fall is here.

Farmers bring in crops.

A farmer uses a big machine.

It is called a combine harvester.

Corn grows in rows.
Combines pick off
the corncobs.

In the Garden

Look at the garden!

It is time to pick

vegetables.

Squash grows on vines.
Find a big one!

Grab a tomato.
Red tomatoes are
ready to eat.

Carrots grow underground. Pull them up.

Cabbage heads
are big and round.

The garden is empty.
What will you plant
next spring?

Glossary

combine harvester—a large farm machine used to gather corn and other crops from fields

crop—a plant farmers grow in large amounts, usually for food

harvest—to gather crops that are ripe

ripe—ready to pick and eat

spring—the season after winter and before summer

vine—a plant with a long thin stem that grows along the ground or up a fence

Read More

Clay, Kathryn. *Farm Machines.* Wild About Wheels. North Mankato, Minn.: Capstone Press, 2015.

Owen, Ruth. *How Do You Know It's Fall?* Signs of the Seasons. New York: Bearport Pub., 2012.

Smith, Sian. *What Can You See in Fall?* Seasons. Chicago: Capstone Heinemann Library, 2015.

Internet Sites

FactHound offers a safe, fun way to find Internet sites related to this book. All of the sites on FactHound have been researched by our staff.

Here's all you do:
Visit *www.facthound.com*
Type in this code: 9781491460023

Index

cabbage, 18

carrots, 16

combines, 6, 8

corn, 8

crops, 4

fall, 4

farmers, 4, 6

gardens, 10, 20

machines, 6

planting, 20

squash, 12

tomatoes, 14

vegetables, 10

vines, 12